My Brother's Gift

Linda Selvey Coyle

authorHOUSE®

AuthorHouse™
1663 Liberty Drive, Suite 200
Bloomington, IN 47403
www.authorhouse.com
Phone: 1-800-839-8640

First published by AuthorHouse 2/28/2008

ISBN: 978-1-4343-4936-1 (sc)

Printed in the United States of America
Bloomington, Indiana

This book is printed on acid-free paper.

Acknowledgements

Gift of Life Organ and Tissue Donation
www.Donors1.org
1-800-Donors-1

For information: Education and Support Services for Donor
Families, Transplant Recipients, Living Donors and Patients waiting
Transplant. Assistance on signing up to be an Organ Donor.

Passing On Smiles ©
B.K.M.F. Foundation 501(3)(c)

Comments and questions for the Author,
please address to the following e-mail:

mybrothersgift@yahoo.com

Dedication

For the blessings of all smiles past.
The pleasure of smiles enjoyed today.
The gift of smiles in the future.

The morning started like most in September, at our house, mom woke my little sister and me up for school. My brother Ryan already left for school, he goes to the junior high. My older brothers, Jack and Bob are out of school and now work. They each work different shifts, so they get to sleep late in the morning. Jack works different days, so sometimes he gets a day off in the middle of the week; I think he's still sleeping this morning. Bob works until late in the night, although this morning he was up getting some medicine, for his headache. Mom drives us girls to school every morning. Sugar is in the first grade and I'm in the sixth grade. Sugar is what we call my little sister, 'cause she's so sweet' - at least most of the time. Dad goes to work very early in the morning, so he is home in the afternoon, when we get off the bus from school.

I really like my school a lot; the teachers work hard to make learning lots of fun. Some of the teachers that taught my brothers are still there. My favorite classes are math and art. Math comes very easy and I can get the work done quickly then have extra time to help other students, as long as we do it quietly. Art class has so many different projects to work on; it brightens up my day. When it comes to reading, it is not as easy; it takes extra time to get that work done. However, I am getting better in reading, because over the summer I joined the reading club at the library.

School went by like a breeze, with only a little homework, extra time to play - 'cool'. The afternoon bus was on time, so me and Sugar got home on time too. Dad finished making us a snack and told us, "Dinner will be a little later than usual girls; mom has a late meeting, but there's a roast in the crock-pot. So, let's plan dinner for about seven, okay."

"Sounds good, daddy." We responded in stereo.

Back in the family room, Ryan was on the recliner watching a ball game and I could hear someone upstairs playing music. Dad went outside to finish working in the yard, when a moment later the phone rang. Ryan answered it, with a brief conversation he went upstairs.

Sugar was telling me about a new book they read in class, when Ryan came back into the room and asked, "Where's Dad?"

With my mouth full, I pointed outside but I noticed he had a strange look on his face.

He came right back inside with Dad close behind, they both had the same look on their face. I wasn't sure at first, what was going on but a feeling in my stomach told me it didn't look good. I told Sugar I would be right back and caught up to Ryan at the bottom of the stairs, "What's the matter?"

Ryan stopped and slowly turned around, "Gracie, I went to wake Bobby up for work and he won't wake up. Jack came down from the third floor talking on his cell phone. I told him I couldn't wake Bob and to please try, while I went to get dad. I didn't know he was on the phone with mom, now she's worried too. Do me a favor and keep Sugar out of this, will you? You can put the cartoons on the television, until I come back down. Okay?"

I really wanted to help but I was so scared, I nodded and added my, much delayed, "Okay."

He was already on his way up the stairs when I finished my sentence, "But tell me what is going on right away, all right?"

"I promise I will come right back and tell you what is happening." Ryan gave me half a smile as his promise then waived his arm as he turned the corner at the top of the stairs. I wanted to say, hurry but it would do no good, he was already in the bedroom and probably couldn't hear me anyway. I turned and went back to go check on Sugar.

In the kitchen, I had Sugar help me put the glasses in the dishwasher then we went in the family room and changed the channel, on the television.

"Oooo, Ryan's gonna be mad at you for changing the channel of the ballgame." Sugar teased.

"Nuh uh. He said it was okay. So there." The sarcasm was out of my mouth before I even realized. Sugar didn't notice anything – but my stomach knew something else was going on.

Even with one of our favorite shows beginning, she watched while I just waited. Minutes were dragging by, the cartoon that I normally liked watching, just seemed stupid. I could hear someone on the stairs and hoping it was Ryan I walked to the archway of the family room. It was, and just as Ryan came around the corner; my uncle came thru the front door. With a quick wave of his hand, he ran past Ryan and up the steps.

My uncle lives up the street a few houses, with my cousin. Now she was walking up the front steps, when she peeked thru the glass, Ryan waved her to come in the house.

"Ryan, what is going on? You promised to tell me." I asked impatiently.

Ryan signaled to my cousin and me to be quiet. Sugar was still in the family room and it was better if she does not hear everything yet. Then he began, "Dad called 9-1-1 emergency."

My mouth dropped open, but nothing came out. Ryan reached over and held one of my hands before continuing, "Dad is on the cell phone with mom right now. She is on her way home from work. Jack and Uncle Ray are still trying to wake Bob - but - he is not breathing normal. That's why Dad had to call emergency."

Ryan barely got that out of his mouth, when the door opened. Officer Bill poked his head in to see who was here.

"Upstairs Buddy?" he asked.

Ryan nodded and with another officer behind him, they climbed the stairs two at a time.

We looked at each other and all of a sudden, Sugar was standing right in between us.

"What's going on? Why are the policemen here? Where they going?" she whispered as she looked up at us.

Ryan picked Sugar up, hugged her and spoke softly, "They are here to help Bobby, he's sick and daddy called the ambulance. It's on the way." Tears began rolling down Sugar's face; her lower lip began quivering, causing all of our eyes to well up.

The other policeman came quickly down the steps, talking into the radio, now we could hear the ambulance siren, coming closer to the house. We were huddling close to each other when dad came down the steps. He came right over to us, "Everyone okay? Well at least you are all together. The medical technicians will be coming right in here and I need each of you to stay out of their way."

I think I nodded but I'm not sure any of us actually heard everything he said. Watching out the front door, we could see the EMTs grabbing their gear and the stretcher, out of the back.

Dad put his arms around all of us for two reasons; a reassuring hug and to make sure we stayed out of the way as he had told us. The EMTs left the stretcher in the living room and carried their gear upstairs. I could hear them talking to each other in medical talk and they were asking questions to my brother or uncle, who were still up there.

All of a sudden, there was no talking, the EMTs were yelling in that medical foreign language and rushed down the steps. Bobby was in their arms, a white sheet dangling as they ran down the steps and put him on the stretcher. The EMTs continued to talk to each other, as if we were not there.

I was so afraid; Bobby's face was very pale. Looking over I saw Ryan covering Sugar's face so she didn't watch. As quick as a blink, one EMT was putting a tube down Bob's throat then covered it with a plastic ball shaped piece, that other EMT began squeezing, in and out on the way out the front door.

Dad's phone rang and he answered it before the first ring finished, he knew it would be mom. Dad stepped away from us, to talk to her; I heard him explaining the EMTs are putting Bobby into the Ambulance. Dad followed right behind them, to find which hospital they were going to.

"Hold on honey." Dad said short - then immediately put the phone to the side. "Where are they going? What hospital?" he called out to whoever would answer.

Officer Bill turned and answered, "Temple, they are going to Temple."

Dad repeated that information to mom on the phone, and then told her he would meet her there.

By now, all the neighbors were out watching, wanting to know what has happened. Dad talked to our next-door neighbor, Mrs. Cind only briefly. Then Dad came in, he announced to everyone, "Mom is going right to the hospital. I am going to meet her there. Mom wants each of us to say a prayer that God take care of Bobby and keep us each strong. So please stay here together till I call, from the hospital, okay?"

"But Daddy," I began to respond but thought not, "Okay" was how I finished.

However, I did stop him instead and gave him a big hug. In mid-hug he whispered in my ear, "Thanks Grace, I will share that with Mom, as soon as I see her at the hospital." Daddy gave me a kiss, and then moved on to my siblings to do the same.

Jack came over to me and spoke softly, "It will be okay Gracie, we'll wait together."

Dad grabbed his keys and out the door, to the hospital.

My Uncle and cousin stayed with us for a while, suggesting we get something to eat. Mom's pot roast was still in the crock-pot. Already having had a snack earlier, we were not hungry now; the roast would have to wait for another time.

My brothers took turns on the house and cell phones, calling and answering calls to and from family members. Grandma and grandpop live down the shore; they needed a call, as well as aunts and uncles also. It was too many to call, so they decided to start a chain, after speaking to my aunts, they called other family members.

I am not the best at waiting so I decided to go back to the family room and get my art box out with some paper and coloring books to work on. It helped my stomach feel a little better and kept me busy until someone called from the hospital.

There was someone on the phone over the next couple of hours; calling because they just found out or they were checking back for updates. Finally the call that stopped the waiting, it was mom. My brothers were on separate phones, while I picked up the extension in the family room, so we could all listen to mom speak, "Bobby is stable - but is in a coma. They are not sure what has caused the problem yet. They are taking some tests; we hope to have some results later. Dad is on his way home to pick you up; Bob is being moved into a room upstairs in CCU."

"What's that?" I whispered to Ryan, who was on the kitchen phone.

"Critical Care Unit, Shh listen."

Mom continued on, missing our comments to each other, "Mrs. Cind will be taking Sugar next door to play and stay over night too. Maybe you guys can get a few things together for her, okay?"

"I'll get it mom, I'm already upstairs." Jack jumped in.

"We can talk more when I see you. Why don't you put Sugar on so I can talk to her?"

I nodded, not sure why – mom couldn't see me, but I put Sugar on the phone.

"Mommy, I miss you. When are you coming home? Are you going to bring Bobby home with you?" As quickly as the questions came out of her mouth, she quieted down, I could see she was listening to mom.

"Like a slumber party? I'll be good, I promise. Good night to you too mommy." "Here, mommy wants to talk to you." The phone dropped to the floor.

"Hello?" I asked.

"I'll see you soon, dad is on his way." Mom whispered back.

"Okay mom, see you."

Mom only spoke for a few seconds, but I could hear it in her voice – the fear.

At the door when Daddy pulled up, I ran to him ready to hug. We exchanged hugs, and then he gave me a little smile and asked, "Can you help me Gracie? Mommy needs a few things, some other clothes; she's still wearing her work clothes. How about getting her sweat pants, shirt and sneakers and put them in a bag. I need to go over and talk to Mrs. Cind, ok."

"No problem Dad. I'll get it."

With a wink from daddy I ran into the house, my mind was racing thru mom's clothes and what items to pick. Up the stairs to my room first, grabbed my pink overnight bag off the hook. It was plenty big enough for what I needed. Zipped over to mom's room, I had to look around to find her sage green pants that are as soft as down. The soft white shirt and comfy shoes were next in the bag, packed up, zippered and ready to go.

Coming down the steps, I could see the ribbons from my sister's ponytails flying behind her as she ran with her friend next door. Dad was watching and waving to her as they went in the house. The brothers came out from the kitchen; it looked like we were all ready to go to the hospital.

Click, click, click went the seat belts before mine – click. Tiny drops of rain started to land on the windows as our car backed up, and then pulled out of the parking spot. The drops of rain got larger the further we drove and closer we got to the hospital. The drive was only about five minutes, but finding a parking place took much longer. All I could think was there must be a lot of people in this hospital. A funny yellow car was pulling out very slow, maybe because the rain was getting harder and it made it more difficult to see. Dad had enough room to pull into the space and I said, "Prepare to get drenched, boys, the lobby is not very close."

Entering the lobby, I looked at my dad and brothers and started giggling because they looked ridiculous. My appearance would be in the same vein. I spied restrooms, pointed and ran to dry off. Lucky for me the ladies room had a hand dryer so I could blow-dry my hair, but afterwards I didn't look much better.

Back in the lobby, I met dad and brothers; together we went to the elevator and pushed the up button. The doors of the elevator opened and a dozen people unloaded before we could enter and press the number 3 button. The critical care unit is on the third floor, when the doors opened it was very quiet. Turning the corner, I saw the family waiting room; all the walls are glass so you can see everyone inside. Out of the room came a bunch of people who all looked like they might be related, most were crying. I was glad they were leaving, it made me sadder and that sick feeling in my belly was coming back stronger.

Standing with my brothers, we waited at the doors while dad went to Bob's room and got mom. The big brown doors that separated the hallway from the critical care unit had small windows to see someone coming out. Within a minute or two, mom was coming thru to my side.

The hug I gave mom wasn't enough to make my stomach feel better, but it would due since everyone needed to hear what was going on. Subsequently, we went back into the family room and sat down. Jack and Ryan sat on either side of mom and put their arms around her and I kneeled in front of her with my hands on her lap. Daddy sat close and looked on, but I don't think he actually saw anything. Sitting quietly for a moment, Mom took a second to look at each of us and her hands gently caressed our faces. I never saw that look in my mother's eyes before and it took until much later for me to realize just what it was I saw.

"I love each of you very much," is how mom chose to start her monolog.

"I have a lot to tell you, but if there is anything you don't understand stop me and ask, okay?" Mom was looking at me first, being the youngest one here; I nodded.

"Bobby is in a very deep coma. The pulmonologist is very concerned because Bobby is not breathing on his own; he is connected to a respirator. The respirator is making sure he gets enough air in his lungs; a tube in his mouth connects to the machine. Another concern the doctors have is that they are not sure how long Bob was in bed unable to breathe normal. Dr. Fitzsimmons is the primary pulmonologist; he or one of his partners will be the doctors coordinating the tests and medicines with the other doctors. Besides the respirator, there are other tubes, wires and machines Bobby is connected to."

"Mommy," I hesitated then asked, "What is a pulma – pulmono - -"

"A pulmonologist is a doctor who diagnoses and treats lung problems."

"And how many doctors are taking care of Bobby, Mom?"

"Well," she started, then thought a moment, "Including Dr. Fitzsimmons, there are four doctor groups working together. There are several departments in the hospital that are involved with testing and there are many nurses. Dr. Bemus from our family group has been here to see Bob and talked to me, for a few minutes. The other doctor groups include the neurologist and the cardiologist."

"Dr. Cantor came in to do the first neurology examination; she let me stay in the room so I could ask questions and understand the process a little better. Either her or her partner Dr. Anacanal will be ordering tests, also. Dr. Siadel is the cardiologist; he stopped to explain that the technicians would be in hourly to run EKG reports. I want you all to know there is a lot of activity going on to take care of your brother."

"Unfortunately," as the word came out of mom's mouth, a tear ran gently down her face but she continued, "None of the doctors can tell us when Bobby will wake up. I have been in there talking to him, so he knows he is not alone."

More tears rolled down mom's face, as they dripped off her jaw little wet stains collected on her blue blouse. Looking at her blouse, I could feel wet trails running down my face, with pools in my eyes, causing my vision to be blurry. I could see just enough to see Dad and my brothers eyes all filled up with tears too.

Dad walked across the room to grab a box of tissues, then made a hand signal hooking his thumb to indicate to mom he was going into the CCU to sit with Bob. Mom nodded slightly as Ryan asked, "When are we gonna be able to see Bob, Mom?"

"Right now they are limiting how many are allowed in the room at one time, so we must take turns. I am going to take Jack back now, and then I will be back for you then Gracie, okay honey."

Again, we nodded as if mute.

I wasn't happy about waiting again but it looks like this is something we might be doing a lot of here. This is a good opportunity to ask Ryan, "Hey, do you know what those other two doctors do, that mom was talking about?'

"What the neurologist and cardiologist?" He wanted clarification, so I just nodded. "Well, they are both specialists you know. The neurologist takes care of all the stuff related to your brain and the cardiologist takes care of the heart. You should know that, dad goes to Dr. Siadel."

"Oh, I didn't realize that. Thanks, I didn't want to keep interrupting mom."

"Don't worry Gracie, I don't really understand all the details either, but I am sure the more information mom and dad find out, they will let us know."

It was understandable that Jack went back to see Bob first; for a couple of reasons; first he is the oldest, and second, my oldest two brothers have a different dad than me. Some of mom's friends referred to Jack and Bob as Irish twins since they were so close in age and they looked alike.

However, having a different father than the rest of us and being ten years older gave Jack and Bob a different bond. Mom married their dad when she was young, but when the boys were very little he left. I don't know all the details; none of us really talk about it. Other than, mommy was divorced and had to raise the boys by herself for several years, was generally the extent of the story. Mom said it was really hard and if she didn't have such a supportive family, she is not sure how she could have gotten thru it. 'Sisters and brothers are a gift God allows your parents to give you' is one of mom's quotes. Mom's original sayings must have come from somewhere deep in her heart. As nice a thought that it is, I found it hard to think of my siblings as gifts *all* the time.

Mommy met daddy a few years later, fell in love and got married. Sounds like a fairy tale but it had to be a little weird for my brothers in the beginning, since they call daddy by his real name, Joe. Also, my brothers have a different last name but again mom and her sayings states 'our hearts have the same family love', and that's what's most important anyway. That one I can agree with all the time without a question.

Back to the reality of the waiting area, it had magazines on all the tables, but they were not really for kids or new either. I paged thru a few, they showed lots of famous people but generally nothing to hold my interest. The hallways showed a greater interest, I found myself wandering around, which ultimately the adventure was useful too. The restrooms were found down the hall to the left, both men and women. There was a water fountain between the entrances of the restrooms. Past the elevators was the door to the stairs and a double set of doors led to yet another hallway. Boredom led me thru those doors, down two more hallways and my choices ultimately escorted me right back into the family waiting area.

My venture was a mere distraction to pass time; it did help some because when I came back to the family waiting area there were extra people. Looking for Ryan, I found a couple of my aunts, an uncle and a few cousins had come to wait with us. All of whom were talking almost at the same time. I heard one of my aunts say that grandma and grandpop were packing a few things to stay overnight. They will be on their way, first thing in the morning.

Many emotions ran thru that room, some looked afraid with others holding tears back by giving hugs. I was squeezed into a bunch of hugs with reassurances of 'everything will be okay' and 'don't worry Gracie'. Hugs are great anytime but what made me worry was those reassurances. Why is it that when someone tells you not to worry the first thing you do is worry? I guess if I had the answer to that I would be grown up or a millionaire or both.

Seeing thru the glass walls, there was Jack coming out from the CCU, wiping his eyes and walking down the hallway towards the men's room. Mom was close behind him but came into the waiting room; she was captured into massive hugs from her sisters and brother. Many tears surrounded her but I guess she was out of tears for now, mom just looked really tired. Her blue blouse, caught my eye, it showed the rings from her earlier tears when I realized she never changed her clothes. I grabbed the bag with her things and turned to face her, that was when I saw her talking to Ryan and pointing to the CCU. He quickly went thru the big double doors and was gone by the time I got to mom.

"Mom, I brought you some comfy clothes and I found where the ladies room is, so you can change your clothes. There you can freshen up a little, and then maybe you can take me in to see Bobby?" I asked gently because she looked so exhausted.

"Oh Gracie, that sounds like the best idea I have heard in awhile." Mom opened the bag I handed her, looked up at me with a tired smile, and replied, "Let's go."

I took the bag to carry and held mom's hand to direct her to the women's room, not far down the hall. When the restroom door closed behind us, an echo vibrated thru the room, it was quite deafening. As mom turned on the water and tested it for a warm feel, the little bit of splashing also echoed in the room. I began taking out her fresh clothes and placing them on the counter.

"Mom, I really want to see Bobby, but I'm scared. Will he know I am afraid even if he is asleep in a coma?" I asked nervously.

"No sweetheart. Bobby won't know you're afraid. We are not sure he can hear us, but there are some doctors that believe people in a coma can hear."

Mom un-buttoned her blouse, took it off and put it in the bag before talking again.

"Now is a good time to remember the funny stories Bobby told you, to help you keep good thoughts. That is really hard to do – I know. As you say your prayers, ask God to keep you strong, to help Bobby any way you can."

Standing up after tying her shoes, Mom looked in the mirror, stretched out her arms and said, "Nice choice of clothes wouldn't you say? I look a little better now, agree?"

"You look mar-r-v-volous, Mother," I answered in a funny voice, we both giggled at the silliness, which is something Bobby would do.

We gathered everything else into the overnight bag, which we dropped off in the waiting room before heading for the CCU and my visit with Bob.

*W*alking thru those big doors to enter the CCU, hand in hand with mom, I looked around thinking – it rather looks the same as the other side. But within another few steps, that thought went right out of my head.

Nurses and other people in uniforms were buzzing around the main section, in the middle. All the rooms were around the nurses' hub. Each of the rooms had glass walls so the nurses could see the sick people all the time. Scanning the area, I spied dad with his arm around Ryan right in front of us. I squeezed mom's hand a little, anticipating all the stuff she had told me earlier. I could hear beeps and swishes even before we entered the room and a technical person was coming out as we got to the doorway.

Dad turned around and saw us; he pulled Ryan closer to him gently, so we could enter the room. There was Bobby just looking like he was asleep, except of course for all these wires and tubes. Numb was the best word to describe what I felt, scared just wasn't enough. There was a chair on the other side of the bed; mom walked me over there to sit. Apparently, she had sat here earlier because her work jacket was hanging over the back of the chair.

Standing next to mom, I realized my mind was moving faster than I could think. There were so many machines, wires and tubes. Mom did explain all of this, but now that I am here - - it is very overwhelming. What should I do? What should I say? Some machines have many numbers on them, yet others beeped or make a swoosh sound. Each machine means something, but what? Is it good, getting better or worse? Thankfully, mom moved towards the bed, which made my mind stop and pay attention to her. She reached up to hold Bobby's hand, than started to talk, "Hi Bob. It's mom, I'm back just like I promised. Gracie is here too. She couldn't wait to see you."

Mom nodded at me so I would talk. Anxiously I made a few noises; words just would not come out of my mouth. Looking around the room trying to get a grip of my mouth, my eyes stopped at Ryan on the other side of the bed. His head was nodding; his eyes were glancing between Bobby and me.

"It's okay to talk to him Gracie," barely came out of his mouth enough for me to hear. It got me to clear my throat and look at Bobby as I said,

"Hey, yo - it's me. So is this place as good as they say it is? You look like you are sleeping but I don't know how you can sleep in this room with all the noise. If you wake up soon I bet they will turn some of this stuff off." I reached up and rubbed his arm up near the shoulder because there weren't any wires there. Then I remembered to say, "Sugar told me to tell you to get better fast. She's not allowed in here, too little."

I rubbed his arm again but this time it was to reassure me. My mind shouted 'I love you Bobby, wake up please', cause my mouth refused to work anymore.

Mom put her arm around me, half a hug, as if she too heard what my mind shouted. I turned to mom with both arms; in turn, she pulled me close. My face leaned into mom's shoulder, so I could hide the tears that leaked out of my eyes. As I got comfortable in the hug, my ear settled on her chest. For a few seconds, I closed my eyes over mom's heart; it was the only thing I could hear or feel. But like everything else in the last six or seven hours that good feeling didn't last long enough.

The sound of Dad and Ryan talking to each other, including Bobby was what brought me out of my cherished moment of peace. My eyes opened, to the steady hum of the automated blood pressure machine reading vital signs. Scanning the room again, I was surprised that I found myself looking at Bob's right foot sticking out of his blanket. As if he was hot and slid it out [from under the blanket] for air, just like he was home, sleeping. Someone walked in causing the lighting to change and something shiny caught my eye; it was on his toe. I softly moved away from mom and went over to investigate.

Surprisingly without hesitation, I touched his toes and found mom's prayer ring. With my hands still on Bob's foot and sliding the ring around his toe, I looked up to see mom watching me.

"I was praying earlier and thought Bobby could use my ring, but it was too small for his fingers so I found it fit one of his toes," mom explained with a little smirk on her face.

All I could do was smile back at her while I continued to play with the ring on Bob's foot. At some point while touching his dry foot I realized that would have normally caused Bob to wake up or at the very least kick away from my hand. When mom told us he was in a coma, I guess I really didn't get it. Now the reality of the whole ordeal began seeping into my brain and melted the smile off my face.

Jack entered the room and spoke before I noticed him, "Gracie, some of the cousins are asking for you. I can walk you out there if you want."

"Thanks Jack," I said while moving towards him, "if you will walk me out this time I will remember for the next time I go back out."

I stopped in mid stride and turned back to mom, quickly retreating to her, "Is it okay if I go out there mom?" I spoke softly close to her face. She nodded and gave me half a smile. With a big squeeze, I hugged her and whispered, "I love you." Mom replied in kind. On my way around the bed I called to Bobby, "I'll be back in a little while Bob."

I proceeded to dad, gave him a tight squeeze, and told him that I loved him too, into his ear. Turning to leave I asked, "Ryan want to walk with us?"

A slight shrug of his left shoulder triggered dad to respond, "That sounds like a good idea. Here are a couple of dollars you can get a drink or snack from one of the machines, okay Buddy?"

"Okay," was all Ryan said then turned and we began to go out of the room. As we turned the corner at the nurses' station, I looked back to the room to see daddy going over to sit with mom. A doctor stopped right outside the room with a nurse and was reviewing a chart; it looked as if mom and dad were going to have another visitor.

One of the nurses must have been watching me because when I turned to walk with my brothers, she caught my eye. It wasn't much, but our eyes locked for a moment, a friendly smile crossed her face, I returned a small smile than dropped my eyes to the floor. Only a half stride from my brothers, I fell in step quickly to turn the corner and find the big brown doors out of CCU.

Time always seems to surprise me, I want it to hurry up or I find myself amazed at where the time went. Both of those things happened in a relatively short period. Waiting to find some information about Bob, then seeing mom and dad come out of the CCU at midnight. Midnight, could it really be that late –yeah and mom was getting us together again. Although this was a very short directive.

"Dad is going to take you guys all home to get to bed. I will be staying here over night. I want you each to try to get some sleep; I realize it will be tough. Dad will call the schools in the morning so you don't have to get up early. Then we can make plans after breakfast for the day, okay?" Mom looked at each of us, to see if there were any questions.

"Okay then, give me a kiss good night."

"Good night mom," I said as I gave her a kiss and hug.

"Good night ma," my brothers said at the same time, they even hugged her at the same time. Dad went over to kiss mom good night too and I heard him say, "Your sister is going to stay with you tonight. She just went to get some tea for you and something to eat. I love you; call me a little later okay, Honey."

We all walked over to the elevator together, we got in and I pushed the button numbered one. Mom was putting her jacket on as the elevator doors closed.

The elevator doors opened to the hallway, and the lobby that was so busy just a short time ago, was very quiet with a janitor wiping the floors and the security guard at the front desk. We found the parking lot half empty with the ground still wet. I was grateful the rain had stopped.

The ride home was the most quiet ride that I ever can remember. Once in the house it didn't take long for everyone to change into pajamas. Goodnight's with kisses and hugs were given to and from each of us. At some point, the night took over and I did fall asleep but I have no idea what was the time.

The yawn happened before I opened my eyes or even realized I had fallen asleep and then my arms automatically took over and stretched. My eyes didn't want to open; they had little crusty crystals left over from last night's tears. Slowly, my eyes opened with a little help from my fingers rubbing the crusties away. The morning light from the window was a welcome change to yesterday's rain.

The house was unusually quiet except for the faint sound of the news from the TV or radio down in the kitchen. Within a few minutes, the smell of coffee made its way to my nose as I walked to the bathroom with my clothes ready to shower.

The shower was longer than usual, probably because Sugar wasn't walking in and out of the room every minute rushing me. I must admit, I did miss her and her daily routine. I didn't realize how much I have become used to her morning ramblings and excitement. I finished getting dressed and blow-dried my hair before going down stairs.

As I rounded the bottom step, a pink patch caught my eye next to the couch. I walked over to check it out; it was my overnight bag with mom's dirty clothes. That was curious; I didn't remember us bringing that home last night. Hearing someone walking around in the kitchen, distracted me, from the bag. I figured it must be dad having some morning coffee. But to my surprise, it was Jack getting a cup of coffee.

"Hey," was out of my mouth before he even realized I was there. Just mildly caught off guard he replied, "You're up early aren't you?"

"I'm usually up this time to get ready for school. But what about you? You don't get up this early usually – what woke you? I thought you were dad, is he at the hospital?" More questions rambled around in my head, but I let him respond.

"Well, I got back from the hospital a little while ago and that is where dad is now."

I was taken back by his response, "what do you mean —you got back from the hospital a little while ago?"

He came back over to the kitchen table, for some sugar and to sit down, then he looked at me again and explained.

"Well, I could not sleep, so about 2:30 I walked over to the hospital to check on mom and Bob. There was no change with Bob, so I sat and kept mom company, for a bit. I came home just after your dad was getting out of the shower. I told him I would hang out 'til you and Ryan got up, so he could go to the hospital. That brings you current with the information I know. How about a cup of coffee?"

As I looked at him with 'WHAT?' ready to come out of my mouth, I saw him wink at me with a sarcastic smile. My face loosened up and I said, "Okay, got me. I'll just have some cereal. I guess then dad's going to be back to pick us up. What do we have to do, call after Ryan gets up?"

With the coffee mug to his lips to take a sip, I could see Jack nod and hear 'uh huh' hum from his throat. Quiet again found itself as the dominant factor in the house, the voice on the radio announcing the next song a weak second.

It was late morning; Ryan and I were watching something on TV and Jack was dozing off in the lounge chair, when Dad arrived home. He was in the family room and speaking before any one knew he was in the house.

"Hi you guys, what's going on here?"

"Nothing here, what is going on at the hospital?" Ryan asked.

"Basically, there has been no change. Mom and I have met with a couple of the doctors this morning. Each has concerns and they are continuing to run tests again, along with some new tests." Dad told us as he sat down on the couch, laid back and closed his eyes.

"How about mom? What is she doing?" I asked with obvious concern in my voice.

Dad raised his hands and rubbed his face and hair, as if he was washing. Then looked at me and told me that mom is very tired and very concerned. Frustrated was not a word I was expecting dad to use to describe mom, but he did. Hurry up and wait stinks no matter how old you are or why you're waiting.

It was about an hour later by the time we were all ready to go. The noon sky was not as bright as the morning. Dad had one of his stations on the radio for the ride to the hospital. Normally one of us would be complaining to change the channel but it was soothing and eased some of the tension, anticipating the day. My mind went back to Jack saying he walked to the hospital, walking would help me get rid of the butterflies in my stomach. Instead I closed my eyes and got lost in the music, taking in nice deep breaths.

The car backed up and I knew we were there. Merely a few minutes later, we were off the elevator looking thru the glass walls of the waiting room. The only person I knew there was one of my aunts, sitting alone. She stood as soon as she saw us and walked toward us. Hugs and kisses were exchanged before she told us grandma and grandpop were in with mom and Bob. Dad went to join them, before we could sit down the ding of the elevator rang and a group walked off. The whole bunch was family members, aunts, uncles and cousins of all ages. Again, we dominated the waiting room and I could feel the power of family sending good thoughts to help Bobby get better. Unfortunately, it did not make my nausea go away or even feel better.

To see mom come out of the critical care unit, gave me a little relief. Grandma and grandpop followed shortly after mom, their eyes looked very sad but each gave everyone a kiss and hug. I walked over to mom and put my arm around her waist, to be close to her. Mom rubbed my back as we comforted each other a little. After a minute or two she bent down and whispered,

"You can go in to see your brother now if you would like. Jack and Ryan already went in; dad is waiting for you too."

"Okay mom. I'll be back in a while," I whispered back then gave her a soft kiss.

This time I was walking thru those big brown doors all alone. It was ominous and the fear must have showed on my face, three different nurses gave me a double take. I continued my trek past the other rooms when a nurse, the one that smiled at me yesterday walked over to me.

"Hi, I'm Deanne. Is it alright if I walk with you down to Bob's room?" she asked in a soft pleasant voice. I looked up and noticed her hazel eyes, they were welcoming and reassuring at the same time. My response was delayed just a moment, "How do you know I'm going to Bob's room?"

"I'm Bob's charge nurse and I saw you in there a few times. I am assuming you are his sister, am I correct?"

"Yes, there is also another sister. Sugar isn't here, she's only six – too little to come into the CCU. What does that mean, you are the 'charge nurse', what do you do?" I responded as if I knew her for a long time, as friends would talk walking along the sidewalk.

"As your brother's charge nurse, I communicate all the information between the doctors, who have ordered tests or medications to be given. I go into his room periodically to check vital signs, make sure all the meds [that is short for medications] are given on time and the IV's are on the correct programming. I wash him and this morning I gave him a shave and trimmed up his whiskers. I even try to see who comes to visit him and introduce myself, in case they have questions. The critical care unit can be scary to people who have never been in here." She finished up just as we got to Bob's room, looking down at me she smiled and said, "See ya later, let me know if you need something, okay?"

Nodding at her, as she walked away, I found there was nothing else I could say. I realized the closer we walked to Bobby's room the drier my mouth became. This nervous reaction was caused by the anticipation of the quiet tension inside the hospital room.

Turning to enter the room, I realized tension was not a word to describe this room now. My cousin joined my dad and brothers visit with Bob. Each of them was involved in story telling about special times spent with Bob. I was in the room only a minute and found myself laughing so hard, partly because of their laughter. If I didn't know better, I would say I could almost hear Bobby laughing along with us.

This visit with Bobby made me feel much better than the others. Remembering all the fun times, we had together, as a family and separately, sparked my hope to shine a little brighter. I was sure we would get good news to brighten mom's day.

*W*aiting for mom and dad to come out of the CCU to the family waiting area, it began to be busy with family. Aunts, uncles and cousins of all ages showed up out of concern. It was the strangest party I have ever been too. Well, I guess party is not the best term to use but there was so many people milling around talking to each other. For all the talking there was, it didn't seem like much was really being said. It seemed we were trying to trick ourselves from getting more worried about the already stressed circumstances. Bottom line we were hoping for a party to celebrate Bobby coming out of his coma.

If I had a dollar for each person who offered to buy me a beverage or snack, I wouldn't need my allowance for a month. The other thing I thought somewhat weird was, 'don't worry – eat,' --that didn't make sense to me.

Walking around the room and hallway, I caught bits and pieces of conversations. The assortment included: funny tidbits from when Bobby was very little and some other recent stories that incorporated a silly voice imitating Bob. Of course, there were others concerned about how mom and dad were holding up thru this nightmare.

Mom and dad were coming thru the CCU doors, so I walked quickly past other family members, to be by their side. Mom leaned down and asked if I would like to take a ride home with her, so she could shower. We would be coming right back because the doctor we are waiting for is expected shortly.

"I'm with ya, ma." I said and grabbed her hand.

"Joe, you do the explaining to the family, so we can go and be back right away, okay?" Mom said to dad.

"Honey, don't worry and be careful. Do you have your cell phone? So, I can call you if I need you."

"Yeah, I got it. Love you," mom answered and kissed dad on his cheek.

The bell rang and the doors opened to the elevator, I had pushed the button while mom and dad were talking. We moved quickly thru the lobby and to the car, both buckled in, mom pulled out of the parking lot. Dad's music was still on the radio, with any luck we can relax a little, on the way home.

About half way home the cell phone rang, mom grabbed it and answered right away.

"Hello?" mom answered abruptly.

I regretted that I was unable to answer the phone myself, very quickly. The half of the conversation I heard was very upsetting. Mom's voice continued to be more distressed as she spoke,

"I'm not even half way home, why?" She paused to listen,

"What do you mean he's there – they said he wouldn't be there 'til later? Joe, what is going on? I just wanted a quick shower so I could freshen up and try to speak somewhat intelligent to this guy."

Hesitation.

"Fine- I'll turn around and be right back!" She threw the phone across the car and cursed.

"Mom! What are you doing?"

"Oh, I'm sorry Grace. I'm just so exhausted and frustrated. The doctor just got to the hospital, asks for me then went in to see your brother. If they would have told me he would be there this soon – I would have just stayed."

"Please calm down, mom it will be okay." I said it – after hearing all those reassurances and knowing they really didn't make me feel any better – I said it. Looking at my mom, I understood a little bit why we say, 'it will be okay', because feeling helpless hurts too.

"I know Grace, I have faith - things will work out just like God planned. I'm very sorry I lost my temper and said those words. You did not deserve to see or hear that. We can just go up this street and turn around."

"Okay," was all I could say. I didn't want to upset mom anymore and I wasn't sure I knew what I could say or do to ease any of her pain. The ride back to the hospital seemed to take twice as long as the ride home or should I say half the ride home.

Mom parked where we just left, since the spot was still available. The next series of events, almost felt like a dream – I don't remember walking, just getting to the destination. Hurrying thru the parking lot into the lobby, the elevator doors opened on cue, before pushing the button and got us up to the third floor quickly. Directly into the CCU, which seemed quieter than prior visits, the curtain was pulled across Bob's glass wall but dad was waiting for us. Mom slid her arm around me and guided me into the room, past dad with my brothers.

"Where is he, Joe? The doctor?" I heard as I entered past the curtain. I could hear dad mumble something back. I turned, thinking I would be able to hear but by then Dad was pointing into the nursing hub.

"What's going on dad?" Ryan asked.

"Mom is letting Dr. Anacanal know she is back, so they can talk. Her sister is at the end of the nurses' station, in case mom needs some help with medical questions. Until they meet and talk, we wait."

There it was again – that horrible four-letter word, 'wait' – so I sat down. The machines were making their noises, numbers changing, I couldn't stand looking or listening to them anymore. I began trying to block them out, when I noticed legs go by; the curtain didn't reach the floor, which left about three-foot of window where you could see people walk by. Most were legs in scrubs, the medical garments worn by staff. Surprisingly, mom's legs showed up alone then another set, a woman in a skirt. She didn't stay long and just as she left a doctor walked over, I could see the white coat. I tried to listen very hard in hopes I could hear something, but Ryan interrupted me.

"Grace what are you doing?" he whispered keeping Dad and Jack out of the conversation.

"Nothing," is what I said but then I pointed to the legs on the other side of the curtain. We returned glances and then looked back, in time to see another pair of legs. I was sure they were my aunt's legs; she was standing very close to mom.

The ten minutes they stood outside the room seemed more like an hour. The doctor walked away, expecting mom I stood up next to Jack. She must have been talking to my aunt, causing her delay back into the room.

Time froze 'til I saw mom's hand grab the curtain, slide it and enter the room. She slid the curtain back to the wall, as if closing a door. Mom did not look good but continued over to Bobby's bed.

"That was the doctor in charge of Bob's case," she began without looking at any of us.

"He has all the results from the tests and they're not good. There has been too much swelling in Bob's brain, even with all the medicine, they cannot reduce the swelling enough. He has not taken a breath on his own; the respirator is delivering every breath. The doctors indicated there was a brain embolism and all options are exhausted to help him medically."

Mom's words slowed, and then hesitated, her eyes filled up and finally said,

"I am so sad to say, Bobby is considered brain dead."

The tears burst from mom's eyes as she reached for dad first. Jack reacted by covering his face and putting his head down on the bed near Bob's. Ryan stepped away shaking his head, repeating no, no, no. For me all time stood still – even though I could hear my parents cry, my brothers repeat 'it can't be', 'no Bob' – my mind could not grasp the whole picture. The horror of mom's words, tattooed onto my soul and in that second, my life changed forever.

My aunt stayed with us long enough to hug each of us and express her sorrow. She talked very close to mom's ear, hugged her again then left the room. Mom and dad hugged each of us individually, then as a group, we tried to comfort each other.

As the tears rolled down my face, I needed more information; I could not accept or process, what, how, why?! I need help.

"Mom, they said Bob was in a coma, he looks the same – maybe they are making a mistake. Maybe he just needs more time. Please mom."

My mother pulled me onto her lap and hugged me, laying my head on her shoulder. She started to talk but the noise that came from her mouth was scratchy and unclear. Daddy handed her some tissues as he wiped her cheeks with some. She blew her nose and began again,

"Gracie, honey, I asked lots of questions of the doctor and so did my sister who is a nurse. There is only one test left for them to do."

Hope shot thru my body for the second it took mom to finish her next sentence.

"They do that test as verification prior to organ donation," she took a breath and held onto Ryan's hand.

"That is something we must discuss as a family, what would Bobby have wanted? He always gave blood to the Red Cross, every time the card came telling him where the local blood drive was. Jack do you know if Bob signed up to be a donor, on his license?"

Jack cleared his throat before he could speak, "I'm not positive mom, but I think he was. Like you said he always donated blood, since high school."

"Ryan, how do you feel about Bob being an organ donor?"

Taking a moment to wipe his eyes, he looked at Bob first before answering mom, "I'm not sure mom, and I never talked or even thought about it before."

"I didn't either mom. And I don't really understand what happens." I interjected before mom asked me next.

"Well, I don't know everything about it myself, even though I am an organ donor. I never thought I-we would ever be in this position with one of our children."

Mom looked up at dad for some comfort before continuing.

"I will tell you what I do know – I know there are a lot of sick people that are waiting for hearts, livers, kidneys and more, so they can live longer. Their lives are spent in the hospital most of the time, if not all the time – waiting for a chance. When a healthy person has an accident or a sudden health problem, like Bobby, the hope is the family will agree to donate organs to help others to continue a better life."

As mom closed her eyes and took a deep breath, Jack came closer, put his hand on her head, and gently stroked her hair.

"Mom, Bobby was always giving – whether it was blood, a wave or his smile. I believe in my heart, he would want to help others even if he can't be here with us."

Mom reached up to Jack's hand and held it, "I believe the same thing, honey."

Dad with tears streaming down his face put his hand on top of theirs and nodded, "I believe, too."

Looking at Bobby, as if he was going to speak up next – I looked for strength. Bobby was always so strong; I remembered seeing him carry the old sofa out of the house, by himself. As that thought went thru my mind, Ryan speaking interrupted me.

"I believe it is the right thing too."

"Mommy," I looked into her dripping, tired red-rimmed eyes, "I believe Bobby wants to help someone and maybe this is how we can be strong for him. Will the doctor explain the other stuff to us, the stuff we don't know?"

As more tears rounded down my mother's face, she reached to my face to caress my cheek, "We can have them explain everything to us, okay."

I nodded and leaned into her shoulder to hold her close to me.

"Why don't we go out to see the rest of the family before we get the donation information?" Mom looked around to a roomful of nodding heads. She stood slowly, as I eased off her lap and walked over to Bobby. Her hand gently caressed his face and kissed him, before leaving the room.

Coming thru the big CCU doors, you could hear talking, crying, even a few sobs, but as we got to the waiting room doorway, the volume magically reduced. My aunt must have broken the sad news about Bobby. Most of the extended family was there, each of us was met with a hug of concern and reassurance.

Time went by as we exhausted ourselves further remembering special memories of Bobby and sharing them with each other. Mom came over to me, "I think it's time for us to go home Grace. Daddy will be staying overnight tonight. I think it's time we go home and get a little sleep. I spoke with Deanne, Bob's nurse and she told me she will have the information about the donation, for us in the morning."

"Who else will be coming home with us mom?"

"Right now it will just be you and me. Your brothers will get a ride home later. I'll meet you at the elevator in two minutes, after I say good night to daddy." She squeezed my cheeks as she walked over to my father.

I said my own good nights' to the family and friends that were still there. I had just pushed the elevator call button when mom and dad walked over to me.

"G' night daddy, I love you," I said softly as I hugged him. Daddy picked me up and held onto me a littler longer than a normal hug. The ding of the elevator rang as my feet touched the floor.

The elevator doors closed and descended, the walk to the car put my brain into a sluggish fog. We didn't talk in the car at all; we were both exhausted and talked out.

In addition, I knew mom was going to have to talk to at least one more person before we could crash into bed – Mrs. Cind, next door.

Mrs. Cind was standing at the door; she must have heard the car. She met mom near our house, I kept walking to give her a few minutes. Mom was right behind me after I opened the door – that was the shortest conversation ever.

Without talking, we went right up the stairs together, separated at the top, mom to the bathroom and me to my room. I put my pajamas on and went to mom's room. She was sitting on the edge of her bed taking her shoes off when I entered.

"Mom, is it alright if I sleep in here with you tonight?"

"I think that will make me feel better too. Crawl on in there and get comfy, honey. I am going to get a shower and will be right in there next to you."

I vaguely remember mom coming back to bed, but the security of her arms around me, supplied comfort to end the worst day of my life. I drifted into the black void of a night without dreams.

I started to feel the warm cozy softness of the blanket around me before my eyes opened. Allowing small slits to peek open, I could see it was still dark and I was alone. To see the clock, I would need to sit up causing the comfort I felt to be smacked with the reality of Bobby's death. My mind paused hoping that nightmare was only a bad dream.

I could hear voices quietly sharing, but the mourning doves were closer and cooed louder than the voices. The doves gave me a clue that it was closer to the morning than I could see. Rolling over and opening my eyes all the way, gave perspective to the glint of early light out the window.

Okay body, let's get moving, I told myself half-heartedly. My body followed as commanded, a quick stop to the bathroom, then to my bedroom for my robe and slippers. I couldn't tell if my chilliness was from fall making an appearance or just me on the inside. Either way the added attire took the chill away.

Descending the stairs, the voices became clear and identifiable, Mom and one of her sisters. Coming around the bottom step, I noticed we had other company sleeping on the couch and love seat. Quietly I proceeded to the kitchen and mom met me with morning greetings and questions.

"Gracie, what are you doing up so early? Did something wake you?"

"I'm not sure what woke me, but once I heard the mourning doves I couldn't get back to sleep." I replied and kissed mom on the cheek and then my aunt.

"We are just having some tea, the water is still hot. Would you like a cup?"

As I walked over to the cupboard for a mug, I replied, "Yeah, but I will get it myself."

The sisters continued their conversation; it was general stuff, nothing important. I pulled the chair out to sit between the two and could see mom did not look much better than last night. Eyes still puffy and red, she couldn't have slept very long. I had some questions for mom but wasn't sure how to start – so I decided to just speak up.

"Mom, did you speak to daddy yet?"

"We spoke a little while ago; he got a little sleep on the chair in Bobby's room."

"Dad can sleep anywhere – that's not a surprise." I hesitated then shuddered a little, "Uh, well – what about the lady who is gonna talk to us about the organ donation? What time do we have to be there?"

"The woman will be there when we get there; time was not to be a worry."

After answering me, mom looked down at her hands, that she was wrenching together. I could tell she had more to say, so I decided to stay quiet for a few minutes. It wasn't that long when she looked over at me to continue, "You know Grace; we have not talked to your sister Sugar, yet. Mrs. Cind told me she would bring her home first thing this morning. Knowing Sugar, she could be awake almost anytime now. I would like to know your thoughts about talking to her."

"I know she is little, Mom, but she loves Bobby. Is there anyway she can go with us today, to see him?"

Mom nodded so I continued, "I think you should just tell her. Then we can go to see Bob together and she can at least talk to him - like we did."

"Don't you think she will be afraid to see him?"

"Mom, I was afraid too. But I was really glad I got to see him and talk to him and even play with his toes. We're all afraid, but it's Bobby and we love him." I choked the last few words out before hanging my head down and let the tears fall into my tea. Mom came over to me, kneeling next to my chair and hugged me. I could feel her tears drip onto my robe. We clung to each other for several minutes until I was in need of a tissue.

"You are a good daughter and a wonderful sister, Grace. We will do this together with Sugar; let her have time with Bobby. After that, we will meet the woman about the organ donation with dad and your brothers. Okay?" She squeezed my hand at the end of her question; I squeezed back and gave a smile.

The timing of our talk couldn't have been better. We had just picked up our teacups when Sugar came zooming in the house. She kept coming thru to the kitchen when she saw mom.

"Mommy," her arms went around mom's neck as she hugged tight, "I missed you so much. Who is that sleeping in the other room, I can't tell, it's still dark in there."

"Well I missed you too. There are a couple of your cousins sleeping; they stayed instead of driving all the way home. Would you like a cup of tea with the girls?"

"Yes, please. Is Bobby home yet?"

"No, he isn't. However, we are going over to the hospital to see him together. Let's take our tea in the family room, so we can talk. Okay?"

She nodded carefully while picking up her mug and turned her head to me and my aunt, "You coming too?"

My aunt told her she was going to get dressed and would be back. I started to get up with my mug of tea and nodded. Mom and Sugar walked into the family room and sat on the couch, I took over the rocker with the big cushions.

Sugar's tea was on the table before Mom began talking to her about Bobby. I listened as Mom found the words to tell my little sister, that our brother would never come home again. Listening triggered a stream of tears to run down Sugar's face- she couldn't believe or understand all of what mom was explaining. I truly understood how my little sister felt. The whole situation was unreal. It was so hard to imagine this was happening to our family – This kind of thing happens to other people. I grabbed some tissues and joined them on the couch.

We tried to comfort each other with hugs and back rub until Sugar climbed on to mom's lap. Unfortunately, we can only do so much, when your heart aches beyond anything you have ever known.

I heard a noise in the kitchen, putting my hand on my mother's back, I told her I would be back. Proceeding to the kitchen to investigate, I found Ryan with his back to me eyeing up the contents of the refrigerator.

"Gd' morning" speaking softly as I walked closer to him, "what time did you guys get home?"

Ryan turned with his hands full with breakfast ingredients, walking to the counter he replied, "It was late, didn't sleep much. Where were you?"

"I was in the family room with mom and Sugar. Sugar just got home this morning; I stayed with her while mom talked to her about Bobby."

Our eyes met for a long moment of silence, and then he continued to get the breakfast items together.

"I didn't think Sugar would be home so early, how she doing?"

"I guess about the same as the rest of us. She is still in the other room with mom. Do you want help making breakfast?"

"I am going to start with the bacon, if you would get the mix together for the pancakes that would be good."

As 'okay' was coming out of my mouth, Sugar came in the room, saw Ryan and called to him. He knelt down to meet her hug, they held onto each other for several minutes, although I didn't hear what they said to each other, they did exchange whispers. After separating, Ryan invited Sugar to help get breakfast together with us. Quietly she agreed and opened the drawer for the eating utensils. Mom on the other hand indicated she was going to shower and finish dressing.

After she left the room, I heard her talking to someone, figuring my cousins were awake and hungry I doubled the amount of mix for pancakes.

The kitchen became alive with bodies setting up, cooking, eating and even laughter. The laughter surprised me but it did feel good to have a few minutes of normalcy. I hurried up the stairs so I could finish dressing, after being the last to complete my meal. Everyone was almost ready to go to the hospital.

Making a choice of the three cars driving to the hospital, I picked my cousin's – since I never had a ride in his car before. We all met in the hospital since the parking lot was almost full, each of the cars was parked in different parts of the lot.

We all got into the elevator, which filled it, and we proceeded to the third floor. Sugar was unusually quiet, at least until we got off the elevator and she saw dad. She ran to him while calling out, landing on his chest, in a hug. It brought tears to my eyes, along with most everybody around me. Greetings and hugs were exchanged with family and friends already at the hospital. My family stayed in one big hug. Before mom and dad took Sugar in to see Bobby, they directed my brothers and me to come to the room in about five minutes.

Each of us milled around until Jack gave Ryan and I the nod, meaning it was time to go. Going thru those big doors triggered my stomach to become very nervous. We walked close to each other down the hallway and around the nurses' hub. Looking around I noticed Deanne watching us go to Bobby's room. She gave me a half smile and nod to remind me of our earlier talk. I returned the nod but I don't think I could move my mouth even for half a smile.

Entering the room, we could hear Sugar whispering to Bobby, as if she was telling him secrets. Once she realized we were in the room, she gave him a kiss and climbed down from his bed. We stayed very close to each other, in fact each of us was holding onto another member of the family. Quietly we all stood supporting each other, I noticed Deanne stop by the door and nod to mom. I figured it was time to meet the organ donation people. Within a minute, mom turned to Sugar and told her we had to go to a meeting in another room and she could wait in the family waiting area with her cousins. Sugar hugged mom and we could hear her say,

"Okay mommy, but will I be able to see Bobby one more time before I leave?"

"Yes, Sugar we will come back to say good bye before we leave", tears began rolling down our cheeks; we left the room.

Mom walked Sugar out to the waiting area and Deanne took us to another room. It was a small room with a long table and a bunch of chairs. Deanne said she would be right back with my mother. It was only a minute later when they walked into the room, behind them entered a couple of other women. Once mom sat down with us, Deanne sat at the other end of the table.

The other two women came around; one sat near mom, and the other stood on the other side of the room. The first woman introduced herself as Aubrey, the other woman's name was Jane. Aubrey is the donation coordinator for this area.

She began, "We are very sorry for your family's loss," she indicated to the woman standing, who nodded in agreement. Turning back to mom and looking at each of us as she continued, "I am here from *'The Gift of Life Donor Program'* to answer your questions about organ donation."

"Well," mom started, "can you explain about it, then if we have questions" her voice drifted off to a whisper.

"We can begin that way," Aubrey said and then continued her dissertation, "with some facts about organ donation. Presently there are approximately 90,000 men, women and children in need of heart, kidney, liver, lung and pancreas transplants. More than 4400 people waiting in the *'Gift of Life'* region alone. Most people support organ donation but less than thirty percent have actually signed a donor card or discussed it with their families. Only a very small percentage of deaths have the potential to donate, of those only about half actually do. We are here due to the unfortunate prognosis given to you about Bob. Given the information we received, at this time we believe Bob to be an excellent candidate to donate. I will be glad to answer questions if someone has one now."

"I have one." I spoke louder than I intended, which made my face turn red and I hesitated before actually asking the question.

"The doctors said Bobby was in a coma and now they say he is - - brain dead," I had to stop to catch my breath.

"But he looks the same as he did when I first saw him. How do they know for sure?"

"Grace, that is a very good question and important. When a patient is in a coma he is unconscious caused by disease, injury or poison. That patient is incapable of sensing or responding to anything that happens around him. Brain death is similar in most ways; the difference is that the central nervous system has no activity. The central nervous system is our brain and spinal cord. The test used to measure brain activity is the E.E.G. This test along with others is used to check breathing and other vital reflexes. When these tests are done over a period of time, doctors will pronounce the patient brain dead. We make sure these tests are run again prior to organ donation. Did I answer your question?"

I did understand - I just could not get my mouth to cooperate, so I just nodded.

"If you give permission for Bob's gift of life," Aubrey again gestured to her co-worker, "Jane will stay with Bob thru the whole process. She will be his voice and protector, to make sure he is treated with respect during his giving process. Jane will stay for all tests and surgery, since your family is not permitted to attend. Nothing will be done that you do not give permission to."

Mom asked, "Basically there are papers for me to sign to give permission for the donation, is there anything else we would need to do?"

"No ma'am, after you sign permission, we will proceed with all other needs. The program will pay for all the expenses related to the donation including surgery."

"If you could give us a few minutes, before I sign the papers," Mom said. Aubrey nodded and stood up, gesturing to Jane and Deanne, the three women left us alone.

Mom wiped her eyes and face before beginning, "I believe we all agreed to the donation last night. Did anyone have any questions or comments we should discuss further?"

"I think she explained everything very well. I do believe Bob would have wanted this." Dad added to the conversation.

Jack spoke up, "I'm sorry – I forgot to tell you I found Bobby's license this morning and he did sign up to be an Organ Donor. We never discussed it but I guess he just figured that would be enough."

Ryan was glad to hear that, I heard him whisper 'good'.

Mom looked my way and raised her eyebrows as a question.

"I am glad Jack found that, but I feel better because what she said about 'Bobby giving a gift of life'. I didn't think about it that way before. Jane is gonna be his protector like an angel while he is giving."

My eyes filled with tears and I bit my lip, so I could continue, "This is his gift – people we don't know will be saved and he can live on in our hearts and memories."

I couldn't talk any more 'cause the tears took over. But I wasn't alone or afraid, my family was hugging me. And I know Bobby was right there helping me understand. It took a few minutes to get ourselves together; apparently, tears are very contagious.

Dad told us that we could wait out in the family area, while mom signs the papers. He figured it would not take too long and we could be out there with Sugar. As the three of us left the room, the women and Deanne picked up a folder and walked towards the room. My brothers put their arms around me as we walked out of the CCU.

Joining the rest of our extended family broke some of the intensity. We were each greeted with a long loving hug from an aunt, uncle and grandparent. Melting into those arms our grief triggered streams of tears that flowed around the room.

Comfort was beginning to creep back into my body when mom and dad walked into the room. It looked like they also took time to grieve with each other. Eyes red rimmed and glassy they were welcomed into loving arms.

Over the next few hours, more family and friends came by to visit and reminisce. Laughter again found its way into my heart and ears, with stories and visits with Bobby.

On one of my treks past the nurses' station, I saw the donor ladies on the computer and phone. Deanne saw me watching, and walked right over, "How you doing Grace?"

"I guess okay. What are they doing now – the ladies from the donor office?"

"They are looking for patients, who are in need of transplants now. They will also be coordinating details, with other hospitals. I would like to tell you, that you have a wonderful family. During this very hard time, your family chooses to help others and honor Bobby's donation. Your brother is a hero."

I watched for a few minutes, eyes glassy waiting until I was able to respond,

"Thanks a lot for watching over my brother. We all - - love him <sniff> very much and we'll miss -<sniff>," with puddles in my eyes I smiled, sniffed again and walked to the waiting area.

Mom and dad were getting my siblings together. Mom spoke up, "we are going to be leaving soon. And I know the other family and friends would like to say 'good bye' to Bob. So each group will get a few minutes, then we will go in together as a family, okay."

The consensus consisted of a bunch of nodding heads. I looked around the room, apparently mom had made her wishes known to all. Each of the families or friends was getting into groups, so they could go for their visit together. Mom walked over to Bobby's friends and let them go first. She continued around the room to let each group know whom they were to follow, in turn.

My brothers and I gravitated to the hallway right inside the CCU doors. We could talk to the group waiting to enter and one of us would walk the outgoing group to the elevator. Mom and dad spent time talking to each group in a random order. Grandma and grandpa with desolation filling their eyes were the last visitors before our immediate family. Mom hugged grandma and grandpa as they exited the CCU, walking them over to sit for a few minutes before going to the car.

Dad was carrying Sugar and holding mom's hand when they walked over to my brothers and me. We walked close to each other; actually, we were all touching someone as we entered Bob's room. As awkward as this experience felt, I looked at Bob's face and it was so serene, it gave me some comfort. Daddy put Sugar on the bed next to Bobby, so she could talk to him, while the rest of us spread out around the bed. That is when I noticed Bob's foot out from under the blanket. Mom's prayer ring still on his toe; there were many prayers being said around this ring.

After Sugar climbed down, the rest of the family took a turn saying our own 'goodbyes'. Sugar on the other hand, took turns being held by the rest of us, that was enough of a distraction for private time with Bob for everyone. Mom was last of the group; I watched as she caressed his face, rubbed his chin whiskers and held his face next to hers. I could hear soft whispers but don't know what she said. When she stood up, she announced, "It is time for us to go now; Bobby will be getting ready for his surgery." Turning to face Bob she continued, "You will be in our hearts and memories always, thank you for all the smiles and laughs you shared with us over the years, son." As she leaned down to kiss him again, her tears ran down his face too.

Walking out of his room, Bob was given a last kiss and final word from each of us. I cannot say I saw anyone as we left the CCU, my head was down and my eyes were puddles. Jack held me close as we walked past the big brown doors into our lives without Bob. Grandma and Grandpa waited for us, to walk to the cars and go back to our house together.

Our home was overflowing with family, friends and food, lots of food. Preparations for the funeral and Mass will wait until tomorrow, after Bob has given his final gift, the *gift of life*.

About the Author

Linda Selvey Coyle born and raised in Philadelphia, PA; comfortably into her forties; she has four children and a husband, who are the love of her life. Grateful for a large family, she now includes two grandchildren, to her blessings.

Drawing, sketching and painting are her talents and passion since her youth. Today, she finds writing a creative release to share the reality of life.

www.ingramcontent.com/pod-product-compliance
Lightning Source LLC
Chambersburg PA
CBHW021250280526
45784CB00005B/2314